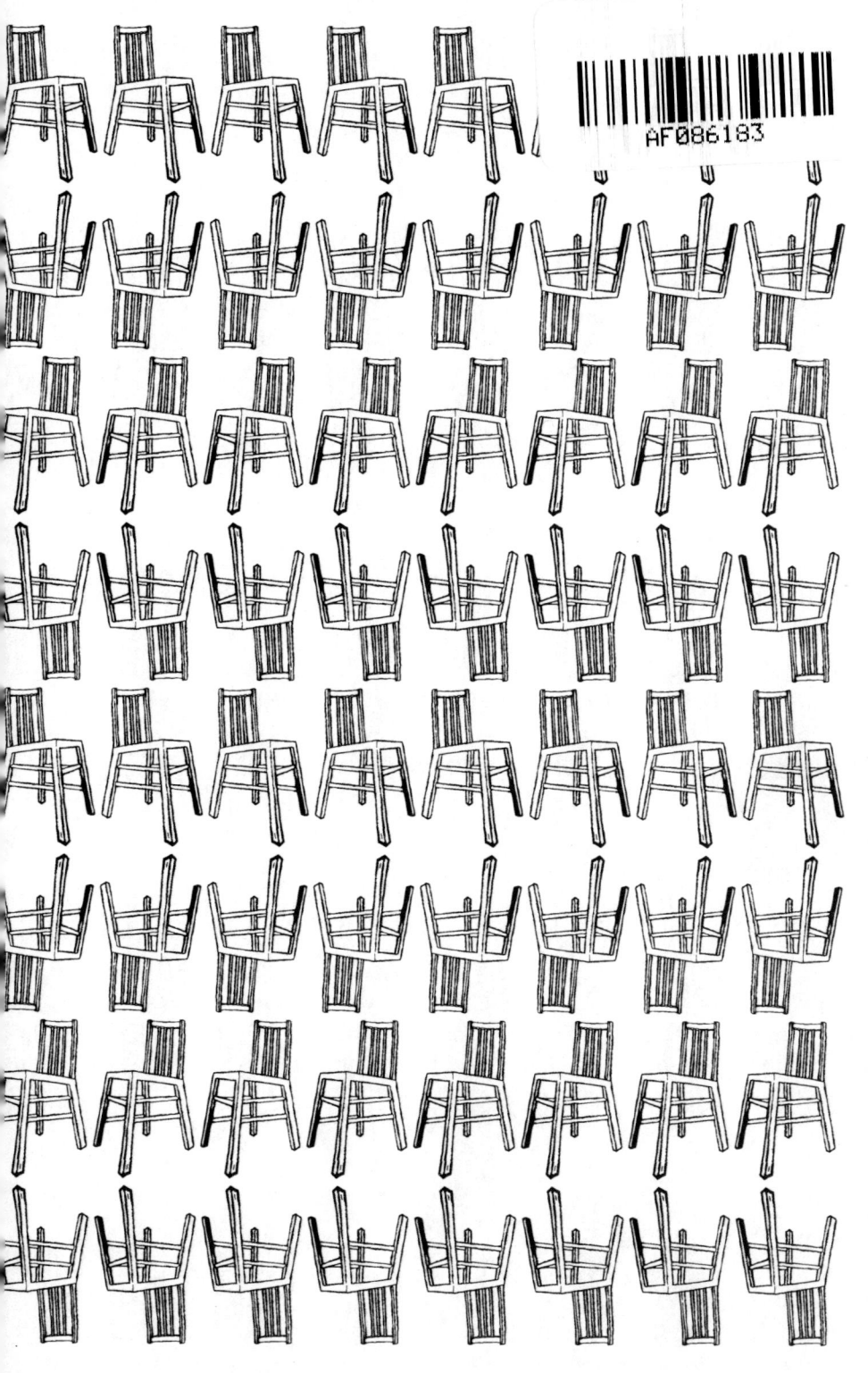

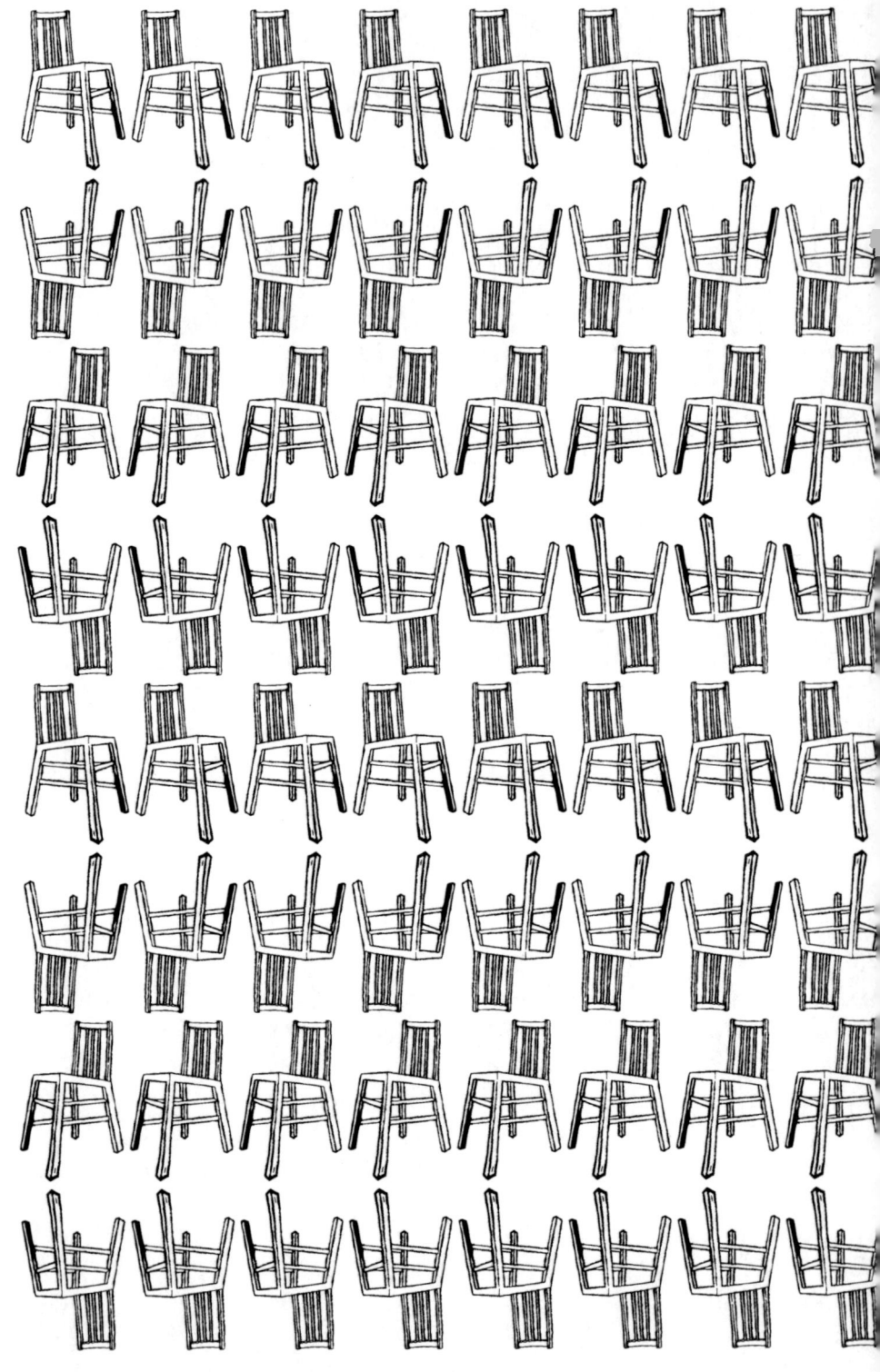

NOTEBOOK IN HAND

First published in 2012
by Stonewood Press
97 Benefield Road, Oundle PE8 4EU
Tel: 0845 456 4838
Email: books@stonewoodpress.co.uk
Web: www.stonewoodpress.co.uk

All rights reserved
© Preface; Martin Parker, 2012
© Poems; estate of John Rety, 2012
© Foreword copyright, Stephen Watts, 2012
© Afterword copyright, Emily Johns, 2012
The authors assert their moral right to be
indentified as the author of their work

ISBN: 978-0-9569122-1-3

Distributed by Central Books
99 Wallis Road, London E9 5LN
Email: orders@centralbooks.com
Tel: 0845 458 9911

Printed and bound in the UK by the
MPG Books Group, Bodmin and King's Lynn
Designed and typeset in Bembo 11pt/12.5pt
by Martin Parker at www.silbercow.co.uk
Cover illustration by Martin Parker

JOHN RETY

Notebook in hand

New and Selected Poems

Selected by Martin Parker

With a Foreword by Stephen Watts
and an Afterword by Emily Johns

CONTENTS

Preface: Martin Parker	7
Foreword: Stephen Watts	9
Alas	15
Six Grand Rooms	17
The Geographer	19
The Meaning of Life	20
The Good Shepherd	21
Tenant	22
The Cherry Tree	24
Vision at 12.30am	26
Work	27
Freedom	28
How Myths are Born	29
Ponderment	30
Vir stultus sum	32
Homageiski to Authoriski of Ulysseiski	33
Monsters	34
Useful to Know	35
To Die in Madrid	36
For Susan	37
Racing News	38
Top of the Morning	39
That was That	40
The Kitchen Chair	41
Tick Tock	42
Conversation	43
Mourn	44
Know This	44
Two Incidents	45
The Boy	46
To My Mother	48

Declaration	49
Understand This	50
His Worldly Goods	52
Terra Incognita	54
Robin	55
Who do we Adore?	56
Georg Heym's Berlin	57
However Absurd	58
The Poet offers His Wares	59
Andrei Cadrescu	60
The Reckoning	61
Advertisement	62
What's in a Word	63
Stone Upon Stone	65
The Door	66
Waiting	67
On the Platform	68
The Would-be Shoemaker	69
Understanding	70
Biology	70
The Journey	71
You Might have Noticed	73
Then and Now	74
Into the Street	75
Some Poets are Even Worse	76
A Moan on a Sunday Afternoon (*The birds sing*)	77
Too Late	78
Contaminated Soil	79
World War Two	80
This is not the time	81
The Question Remains	82
Notebook in Hand	83

Chapter One	84
Chapter Two	84
Chapter Three	85
Chapter Two Thousand and Fifty Seven	85
Martial said it First	86
Running out of ink	87
Progress	88
The Link	89
To and Fro	90
Art Lesson	91
A Moan on a Sunday Afternoon (*There was a tribe*)	92
The Moment	93
There was a Time	94
For Thoreau in Sorrow	96
Art and the Man	97
Where is that Child?	98
Now we know exactly	99
Why two?	100
Up in the Air	101
In the Museum	102
H'onopononopono	106
Foreign Languages	108
Country of the dead by Attila József	109
Two fragments by Attila József	109
Saffron	110
Your Cool Light	111
Perhaps	112
Address Unknown	114
Tongue-tied	115
Afterword: Emily Johns	117

PREFACE

This book is long overdue. The first time I heard John Rety read his own work at Torriano Meeting House in Kentish Town, London, was a true pleasure, and also fascinating – he was a man who didn't seem to take himself too seriously, even though it was clear the poetry was taken seriously, and he enjoyed playing with his audience and encouraging them to play along. On this occasion, he'd prepared a small book from folded paper – an anthology made up of his poems' titles – which he referred to before he read the poem from his collections. A lot of poets make lists to help them remember their reading order, but this was something different – the poems here John saw as fit for being in a book (even if they were just titles). There was the germ of a Selected there.

I came really to know John's poetry through working with him in 2007 on his Hearing Eye pamphlet *In the Museum*. You get to know things about a poet when you design their book with them, and one of the things I learned was that John was fine with the idea of publishing his own pamphlets – and in fact he liked the immediateness of the old school pamphlet; printing enough copies to sell hand to hand, and often giving them away – but he was never very happy about publishing his own full collections. For him, his collections should be books other publishers produced. So when I floated the idea, back in 2007, that John should publish a New and Selected he gave me a typical John look and said no.

But it was an idea that wouldn't leave me, especially after John told me he was writing new material, and so, two years later, I suggested it again. He still refused to publish it under Hearing Eye, but this time he followed the no with a challenge – 'Martin, you publish it!' I said, 'OK', partly to call his bluff but mainly because I wanted this book to happen. This stopped John in his tracks. It wasn't often he was speechless but he was then. It took another minute before he nodded and joked 'you'll have to pay permissions to Hearing Eye.' We arranged a timeline and some meetings and John started to collect his work together – most of it wasn't on disk and had to be re-typed. He handed me the first draft of the manuscript, which included a section of new and unpublished poems, in January 2010. At our meeting I asked him how he felt about the older work and he said that he still stood by it.

John was very fond of telling how Hearing Eye was started almost by accident when he'd suggested to John Heath-Stubbs that Heath-Stubbs should publish some of the poems he'd read at Torriano. A few days later the manuscript was on John's doormat. Stonewood Press is a little bit like this; I'd been thinking about starting a small literary press for many years and this was one of the pushes I'd needed.

Although John handed me the manuscript in January 2010, there was more work to do on it – we still didn't even have a title for one – we both knew this and were looking forward to the conversations. When John died a month later I had a decision to make: do I continue or not. Actually, there wasn't a decision to make; if Susan, John's partner, was happy, then I'd publish these poems. It wouldn't be the book John and I would have put together, but it would be a book to stand by. This would have been impossible without the support of a group of dedicated people, most significantly Susan Johns whose patience and diligence to John's work, at a very difficult time, was invaluable. My deepest thanks to her. I also would like to thank Stephen Watts for his insightful and elegantly written Foreword and Emily Johns for her tender Afterword (and for showing me sides of John I hadn't seen before). I would also like to thank Jacqueline Gabbitas for her encouragement in my choices of poems and their ordering, and Katherine Gallagher and Hylda Sims for their support and interest.

Mostly, I'd like to thank John for this opportunity to finally publish his *New and Selected*, but especially for his friendship.

Martin Parker, January 2012

FOREWORD

'There'll always be Chaos, until Anarchy is restored'

John Rety – or Réti János, writer & publisher, anarchist & pacifist, artist, poet & chess-player, as the invitation to his memorial so movingly put it – was born in Budapest in 1930. He thus lived his childhood years in the repressive atmosphere of Admiral Horthy's extremist regime & his early youth in the deprivations & turmoil of war amid the struggle against the weight of German fascism. While his childhood of course had many influences, this early presence of unfreedom clearly moulded his sense of life values and the poetry he was to write many years later. After he came to London in 1947 – just after his 17th birthday – he was instinctively drawn, particularly from the mid 1950s on, to cultural & political anarchist centres, spending time in the jazz cafes & bohemian bars of Soho and the community halls of anarchist gatherings, involving himself in the 'Committee of 100', the Aldermaston marches & other direct expressions of democratic struggle. Such concerns & places were to remain close to him throughout his life & all these experiences, along with his Hungarian mother tongue, fed into the poetry he began to write after 1980.

While his writing was in and of the last quarter of the twentieth century and the first decade of the twenty-first, his language and its moral commitment go right back to 1930s Hungary, to the emergence of fascism, to his utter concern with freedom *per se*, his experiences in Britain, both urban and rural, from the 1950s on, and his huge commitment to such causes. I think John Rety was always conscious – if not always thinking – of his own bilingualism, the Hungarian that lay behind his English. It is part & parcel of his apparent lightness, almost jokiness, and contains his severity, or at the least the seriousness that was born out of his beliefs and lifelong experience.

He arrived in London not in or after 1956, but as early as 1947, carrying with him a childhood lived through an increasingly rightist regime & teenage years lived through the war. His family was split up during the war and many he never saw again. His own grandmother was shot by a soldier almost after the very last acts of the war – shot for trying to warn the soldier the war was over – and this distressed him deeply. Whether such experience bred in him a love of freedom and a vitality to defend it, or whether such feelings and beliefs were natural to him – and likely both are true – he showed throughout his life both a grave and mercurial concern equally for individual freedom and for collective responsibility.

His poetry always exhibits a lightness, even when dealing with dark gravities, and a clarity where he never lost touch with the serious business of living. He managed to write in ways that at times appeared light but always, always held tightly to freedom. Such attachment can become a heavy weight, especially when a writer is sensitive to ever-repressed freedoms: but Rety's poetry never succumbed to world-weariness, even where that was his subject, or it might be expected to, or where others do.

John Rety also brought his Hungarian language with him, and a love particularly of Attila József & Miklós Radnóti, the former being a lifelong favourite. It is perhaps worth remembering that he was born in 1930, seven years before József's death & fourteen before Radnóti's & that both poets were revered in Hungary, especially in leftist 'freedom' circles throughout the '30s & war years. It is interesting to note that he was wary of translating József and only rarely did. There is a verse from a József poem included in this book, seemingly as a five line translation standing on its own ('Country of the Dead'), and there is one of József's wonderful late fragments:

'the poet is the engineer/of the world's magic'

Treading as they do the appalling line between totalitarianism &

utter freedom, these words perhaps get close to the heart of John's concerns & sense of poetic value.

Rety's attitude to translation is complex. He wanted to have József & others done well in English, but he was certainly wary of the act of translation. At the same time he & I often talked of collaborating on a wider translation of József – and at the end of such conversations, though his drift was certainly 'should we?', he always said 'we must'. It is one of my sadnesses that we never managed to find the time to take each other up on this challenge. It is also worth noting that the Torriano meetings that John initiated & 'presided' over for so many years attracted a good proportion of bilingual poets & poet-translators to an atmosphere of language's fluidity. Other friends, maybe with greater accuracy than me, would want to emphasise the 'Englishness' of his poetry & put to one side the 'adopted' nature of his language. There is some good sense in saying this, since John knew his English poetry widely and deeply, and back to its Anglo-Saxon roots, as the poem 'The Moment' indicates.

But perhaps the best thing would be to emphasise both the adopted Englishness of his language and the bilingual roots of his sensitivity. One of the writers he most admired was the poet & translator A.C. Jacobs & I think that what he most admired were the 'hiddenness' of Jacobs' energies, his wry humour & the ability to translate, and also the creative edginess of being 'foreign' in the language of his writing. In a late poem – written when new legislation made his chosen statelessness no longer admissable – John wrote 'you may see me, comrades,/Dance and dance the anarchist monarchist polka'. This is metaphor for his poetry but also for his life. He published a chapbook & then, with Anthony Rudolf at Menard, a large selection of Jacobs' work & later a CD of his poems & he went out of his way to talk about the man and to promote his work. This was a very real and deep appreciation: such is also deserved in John's case, both the life and the poetry – that he is able to conclude a poem ('Address Unknown') that begins 'Mother, they are killing each other' by saying, without cynicism, if with some irony, 'it looks to me/something might be done about/the state of the world.'

We may tend to think of John as an older man, however much his impish freedom should warn us against this. But there is a full-face photograph of him from the 1950s at a demo, black hair flowing and eyes brim with vitality and wicked humour. We can sense the language of his writing within him then. At the time he was more concerned with a novel and the theatre and then later with such weekly anarchist editorials and *feuilletons* as he was writing: but as he became older he was drawn more and more to poetry, recalling perhaps his first & great love of the poetry of Attila József, and in some way sensing how freedom was rooted, if impossibly, in language. From 1982, when he co-founded the Torriano readings, he wrote fairly continuously until his death, publishing mostly in chapbooks: *Song Of Anarchy & Other Poems* (1989), *Banal Incidents From My First Period* (1993), *A Stranger Here* (1998), *In The Museum* (2007). Through these last years, as he immersed himself in the freedoms & dense risk of poetry, he always carried the young man – his own self – within him.

John Rety's poetry is not as well known as it should be, or as it should in his lifetime have been. It is a little like the gatherings he presided over at Torriano: comradely & warmly open, edgy and troubled and acerbic, usually outside the run of mainstream ambitions and fundings, well known to many and yet totally unknown to many others. That he was a fine chess player, travelling widely to tournaments and representing his chosen country at a senior level, was also a hidden fraction of knowledge. It would be appropriate, and very welcome, now that a full selection of his work is available, were his poetry to be seen as representative of what is open, fine and troubling in English poetry, if he were to be read more widely & recognised for what he gave & did.

As far as we know John Rety wrote no poetry in his Hungarian childhood and youth, neither did he in the first years of his coming to London. Indeed his first poetry book was published in 1989 and he probably wrote little poetry before 1980 or so. He was writing though – a novel, published in 1953, and editorials for the anarchist weekly *Freedom* in the 1960s. He was a contributing editor of the latter at that time, and he continued writing weekly columns for the press, some of which are collected in *Through The Anarchist*

Press (Freedom Press, London 1996). His involvement in British culture in the three decades after his arrival in 1947 was largely in the Soho jazz, music & theatre of the margins & in the rich culture of anarchism that he was immersing himself in. Much of this with his long-term partner of many years, Susan Johns. The lovely photograph of John sometime in the mid-late 1950's, hair black & not yet grey, a young man's wide open smile to the world – in a way it sums him up, but it also evinces his sturdy determination, his deep seriousness & commitment. All these qualities are to be found in his poetry: apparent impishness setting off a deep and complex concern, both for human rights and human folly. And then also in the poetry, his spark of unexpected tenderness.

To fully appreciate his poetry, it matters to realise that in 1982, with Susan Johns & others, he set up Torriano Meeting House, from which regular weekly poetry readings later evolved, and that he convened these readings until his last breath. A wide range of poets sought refuge there, were given poetic sanctuary, graced the Sunday readings or at times felt the edge of John's acerbic, translational wit. He also founded Hearing Eye, establishing a pamphlet series that gave many poets their first publication, where other publishers had failed to notice or to heed, as well as publishing more substantial collections. Among the many poets John published were John Heath-Stubbs, Bernard Kops, Jane Duran, Adam Johnson, A.C. Jacobs, Gerda Mayer, Dinah Livingstone, Jane Elder, Richard McKane, Paul Birtill, Miroslav Jancic, Raymond Geuss, Leah Fritz, Valeria Melchioretto, Anna Robinson & Martina Thomson. He fed many poems into the *Morning Star*, edited anthologies (*In The Company Of Poets*, 2003 & *Well Versed*, 2009) and was himself celebrated with the festschrift *Torriano Nights* in the year before he died. His memorial at the Art Workers' Guild in Queen Square (just a few doors from the Faber building, where most likely – given the sad shared sharding of our little poetry worlds – he remained totally unknown) was testament not just to his popularity but also to his resilient & diverse openness. If so many people gathered to celebrate his memory, it was at least in part because his Torriano was a place of genuine, untrammelled poetic gathering & unsought affirmation.

Life – living and breath – is not of the essence for a lot of poets, but with John it was and his contributions to poetry in London & much wider, under-appreciated by some, were essential & vital. It was a part of his own poetry, of his life as a poet. Although he took himself seriously – I can feel the glint in his eye undermining these words! – he was also very much self-deprecating about his work: but here it is, a rich & wide selection, two years on from his death, full of life-giving freedom and energy.

Stephen Watts, December 2011

POEMS

ALAS

There never lived a poet
who could free himself
from the faults of his age.

SIX GRAND ROOMS

Certainly, there was a door
And no doubt it was on the second floor
Below us lived a tiny furrier with his plump wife
There was a thin girl playing hopscotch
On the landing of a cavernous staircase
Empty of people, though the house was full.
Surely there was a front door
The windows looked out on a busy town's intersection
Four main roads and houses and carts and horses
But there were trams and buses too
And a wind that never stopped blowing.
There was also snow and collapsed horses
But if you crossed the street there were surprises
At every corner, the smell of roasted chestnuts
And great plate glass windows through which
You could see rows of fatmen eating boiled eggs.
Houses upon houses, and always another day
Upon another day with somebody like me,
What they called a boy. How could it have been me
As I can't remember every item or a single toy
Or even the bed I must have lain and slept on;
In which of those six or seven rooms
Plus kitchen and bathroom stood my bed.
What shelf was mine, what books, for surely I could read,
Or if pushed, to write in many smattering tongues,
Some alive, many that smelled sweetly of death.
'Come on, you can do better than that'
There was a table that took a whole year to walk around.
When all of them were in their beds you were able
To spread your things, even to draw a picture of a glass

Half full of water and half full of air.
That was on the dining room table. Did you sleep under it
At night or on a settee in the corner.
You must have eaten something, for you distinctly remember
A disapproving remark, 'Stop slurping!' Whoever said that?
How many years cannot be accounted for, six grand rooms
Almost empty except for the bedbugs marching down the wall.
Not without other snapshots of moments, pictures and sounds
Almost clear in the memory. Each day and each night
A relentless progression. But why me, why should I be
Its only remaining, existing witness of over seventy years ago?

THE GEOGRAPHER

A map made from stones
    Each of its own locality
        Preferably starting with the coast-line

Today I collected nine pebbles
    From nine separate beaches
        Or possibly eight – the ninth could be polished glass

Late in the evening I cleaned and polished the stones
    Painted them with egg white
        And they now shine like stars

They do nothing of the sort
    But they do seem to have a benign
        And reassuring presence.

THE MEANING OF LIFE

You ask me what is the meaning of life
After a long silence I say
'There is no meaning'
You protest:
'But certainly there is life
Shouldn't it have a meaning?'
There is an even longer silence, then
Reluctantly I say, hoping to be helpful:
'Life is a holiday from nothing.
A bit peculiar, I admit'
You say, preposterous, life must have a meaning.
And so the conversation continues.
Soon our holiday will be over and
We haven't even unpacked our bags.

THE GOOD SHEPHERD

He was the good shepherd
With a legendary flock
He tended to them gently
And they followed after
As he took them swiftly
To the lushest meadows
And the pleasantest pasture.
The sun shone, the rains fell
Nature's vestments changed
With alternate shades of sorrow and gaiety
The shepherd strode on
And his flock followed after.
At times he glanced back
His gentle eyes delighting
In all that sky and earth offered
All eternity was there
Mountains, rivers, abundant wealth.
The good shepherd was the best of beings
And nothing could excel his followers.
At times he looked back
And saw his abundant flock
All was well with them
And all was to his liking.
But in all that pleasure
There was a tinge of pain
That whenever he glanced back
He never saw the same creatures.
This brought tears to his eyes
For wherever he directed his gaze
He never saw the same face twice.

TENANT

Oh yes, we can ignore the shouting
Whether behind closed doors
Or out in the open fields.
We can choose our friends
And ignore the problems of
The dirty, the unwashed, the ignorant
And avoid if we can the aggressive
Close our eyes to the outstretched hands
That are everywhere, everywhere, everywhere
Close our eyes to the beggars of the town.
Oh yes, we can ignore the shouting
We can ignore our own pleading,
Our own anxieties.
We are not as bad, not as ugly
Not so stupid as that raving
That undescribably filthy
Oh yes, we can listen to the decent
We can hear what is decent
We can hear the nice noises, the acceptable ones
We can hear the adding machine, the police siren,
The everso friendly voices on the screen
On the pulpit, on the rostrum and on the telephone,
The quick cheery tune that escorts us across the street.
They are sanctioned these voices
Therefore they are good.
Oh yes, we can ignore the shouting
Our lease is duly signed
And our job is secure
Here is your key, now get on with it,
Noon day and night
Secure it tight
Leave on the light

Let them think your hovel is occupied
While you are on a flight
To some exotic sight
Oh yes, we can ignore the shouting
And we can hardly remember
The shouting, the misery, the desperation
All that is of the past
The utter, utter degradation,
Now it is our turn, my turn, my key's turn.

THE CHERRY TREE

In order to write a poem
About a cherry tree
The poet tried to remember
When he last saw a cherry tree.
Perhaps he never saw one
Not for the last few years anyway.
In front of him stood a tree
Which wouldn't do for a simile
He had in mind – a concept
That had something to do with
Spider webs and death
Which he thought would be better expressed
By a simile about a cherry tree
Slim, sinuous, slenderly tall,
Self-sown, somebody spit it out
And now it was growing in his garden.
There were some crinkled green leaves
Full of busy ladybirds –
Which just shows it is difficult
To keep to the subject.
The temptations are endless
I suppose it is the wrong time of the year.
Even if this were a cherry tree
And it wasn't, even if the simile
Could be adapted a little
There can't be many people
Who would object, but
It won't do old shoe.
The poem you had in mind
Was meant to be a simile
About your life, you are one red cherry

And all the other cherries
Are eaten one by one and
You are the last one left
Even if a bit rotten but still alive.

VISION AT 12.30AM

for Emily

From Baker Street to Euston Square
On a rattling hurtling tube train
Early morning very weary
The dirty dozen travelled together
On their way to who knows where
Very weary, very wary
Early morning tempers all
Blackman, hippy, gay and pleasant
On their way to who knows where
Hurtling through the empty stations
Confident and fair.
        I smiled, he nodded, she twinkled
        He nodded, she twinkled, I smiled
From Baker Street to Euston Square
On a rattling hurtling tube train
Early morning very weary
On our way to who knows where
Just as cheerful, just as fair and how
We laughed and smirked and twinkled
(the new jews)
On the last train to Dachau.

WORK

*'...the function of living organisms is merely
the distribution of matter...'* – Bertrand Russell

Philosophers are a rare and valuable commodity
Although the innumerable shops for the selling of merchandise
Are bursting with innumerable products on their shelves
It is unreasonable to expect a busy shop assistant
To find for you just that shade of philosopher you require
And of the right size and substance to satisfy your taste.

This is why it is so much easier to buy cheese.
All you have to do is to point at the wretched stuff
And pronounce clearly: Half a pound, please.
Then eat the stuff and take part, your own part,
In the bodily distribution of matter.

Ah, had you asked: half a philosopher's stone please
You will find well-stocked shelves, right next to the cheese.

FREEDOM

for Philip Sansom

Where is that land
Show me that land
Don't say it never existed
Petőfi, Makhno and Durruti –
Did they all die in vain?
Are we just dreamers and
Abstract thinkers
Don't we know more than that?
What I don't know, you might know
Somebody, somewhere on the wide ocean
Up a high mountain
Where beauty conquers terror
Might still know where
Behind the screen of clouds
– Don't tell me it's only in my mind –
Is that land, the land of the free.
Don't say it never existed

HOW MYTHS ARE BORN

Eve and her apple
Newton and his ditto
The wind is rustling the leaves
Then the turbulence subsides
I am staring at a bucketful of windfall apples
How innocent they look in their shiny green-skin dignity
They and each one plead
We are but symbols of the unexpected.

PONDERMENT

Heisenberg said: 'Observation alters
The phenomenon observed.'
T.S. Eliot said: 'Studying history alters history.'
Ezra Pound said: 'Thinking in general alters
what is thought about.'
John Rety said: 'That gives me a lot to think about.'

Bernard Kops said: Left wing, right wing;
      Two wings flapping
        The same old bird.

Laou Tsze said: 'Confucius, you are proud;
      Sages should love obscurity
      You are vain and ostentatious,
      Sages study time and circumstance
      Before they speak and make
      No parade of knowledge and virtue.'

Laou Tsze also said: If the string is too long,
        It is shortened.
        If there is not enough,
        It is made longer.

Yetton Amed said: Where you are
       There will you stay
       And meet your life
       As it comes your way

Yetton Amed also said: 'Today I listened with attention
To a recitation of numbers
From one to one hundred
There was relief and triumph
As the numbers unerringly
Followed each other
What a feat of memory
And what control, what style
And how the diction changed
As the patiently determined voice
Clambered over each succeeding hurdle
As each number became bigger and longer
What exultation
As it finally reached its destination.'

Epictetus said it first: Remember
That you are
Only an actor
In a play
Which the laconic manager
Directs.

★

Happily the bird chirps on its own accord
And varies the trill to suit its mood.

VIR STULTUS SUM

They took me to task
That I didn't write enough
But when I wrote more
They got sore.

HOMAGEISKI TO AUTHORISKI OF ULYSSEISKI

No horrification is intended
Harticulate the hounds
Choice be plessed
Jamesian Joycean choice be plessed
Great tunabiga thingimob
Who gave dis uplift
When I'mski was downski. In gloomski.
The way Imski understandski
Is diski.
Out of the kindnesses of a well-furnished sole
Came to me the gifty of languageski from this
Marvellouski, geniuski, brilliantski, good humouredski
Goot camaradski Jamesiski Joyceiski authoriski scribleriski
Amazing life-giveriski.
Taffetaffe sounded.
All senses accounted forincluding includingfor touch, smell and taste.
Thankski!

*

      The right word in the right order
      Is certainly an order and a half
      The wrong words in the wrong order
      Are easier   by half.

MONSTERS

I hear them on the radio
I read them in the print
I see them on the telly
But when I look for them
Search as I may
I cannot find them in the flesh
For all monsters, however great
Are changed tame by my proximity

USEFUL TO KNOW

Poetically speaking
Whispers and shouts apart
It is us who hold up the firmament.
Pull out one of us – we wobble.
Pull out a whole generation, pull out
An entire nation, the firmament
Will crack us into smithereens

TO DIE IN MADRID

i.m. A.C. Jacobo

No tears in my eyes
      only
The sudden news of your
      death
But the kind flame of
      candle
The taste of salt and smell of
      wax
Of some of your being
      here
And your words, your
      letters
Illuminate what remains of the
      night
You were right about the
      light

FOR SUSAN

I am looking at a portrait I painted
Of you some sixty moons and suns ago
Your black hair sparkles
Your gentle eyes confront the here and now.

RACING NEWS

I have three horses in my stable
Old as they are, they still gnash their teeth
They are called Bronchitis,
Prostate and Cardiac. Each is striving still
To be the first through the finishing line.
I cannot tell which one will win.
Most likely it will be a photo finish.

TOP OF THE MORNING

It is a good thing this early morning
When the mind is fresh
Until the moment when last night is remembered.
Horrors!
It is good to write when the mind is fresh.
See how through that window a new world pours through.
Last night's shadows lurk in the bushes
Horrors!
Let them lurk, this morning's light
Has blotted out the shadows
It is good this early morning
When the mind is fresh.

THAT WAS THAT

He went out for a cigarette
And came back without his hat
He went out to look for his hat
And came back without his cigarette.

THE KITCHEN CHAIR

Think of the kitchen chair
Then having thought,
Write down what you have thought.
Then having written down what you have thought
Think about the kitchen chair again.
Then having thought about it
Long enough
Ask yourself this question:
Has the kitchen chair changed
In your mind
Since you have written about it?
Read what you have written,
Then sit back and think
And having thought
Write it all down.
This will keep you ungainfully occupied
For the rest of your working life.
They will point you out at the Compendium:
'There goes the man who writes the kitchen chair poems.
Everybody thinks he is the new Maya Kovsky;
If you want my privatised opinion
I am sick and tired of his kitchen chairs –
Kitchen chairs this, kitchen chairs that,
Are there no other chairs in the world?
Chairs of this and Chairs of that, Boardroom chairs,
Chairs of Grants and non Grants,
Chairs bolted down at the DSS – He'll soon find out
And anyway if he wants to make a living out of his writing
There is more money in bedroom chairs.'
Having heard all that, think again, write it all down.
Await no payment, no thanks, no fob watch of olden times.
Clear off and get out of the kitchen.

TICK TOCK

I'm like a clock
Wound up alright
Just that the minute hand
              goes slow
And the hour hand
              goes fast

I have learnt to live with it

But others cannot tell the time
       just by looking at me

A small adjustment is needed
But this is a clock
Nobody knows how to repair
Perhaps it has never told the right time.

CONVERSATION

Have you seen it?
No, I have seen her
And I have seen him
But I haven't seen it

Would you like to see it?
No, I would not
I don't wish to be rude
But I know I would not like it

There is nothing in it
Why don't you try it
You can always leave it
If you find you don't like it

I'll tell you what
What?
If you so much like it
Why don't you have it!

MOURN

Mourn for those
Who no longer know
How to mourn
Or whom to mourn.

KNOW THIS

It is the job of each and everyone
To be able to stand on their own feet
And not on any account on
Somebody else's feet

TWO INCIDENTS

A room. Many people. For a talk.
Arriving late. Such silence.
Peace and quiet. Nobody utters a word.
A rostrum. A table. Flowers in a vase.
Sun-shine pours through the tall windows.
Waiting. Is this the wrong room?
After a while go out into the vestibule
And speak to the attendant.
'Excuse me, but I was expecting to hear a talk
On libertarian education.'
'This is the talk, but you are disturbing everybody.'
Go back. Still not a word. When suddenly
The man arises and talks. Non stop
Words pour out of him for a good hour.
Then he sits down. To complete silence.
The sun is out. Doors open.
Everybody leaves together.

★

More like a barn than a room. A big gathering.
Arriving late. A dark round house hole.
Throng of people. Everyone listening. Watching.
A shaft of light through broken window.
A stage of sorts. Two men. One screams abuse.
The meek other says nothing. Defenceless.
Going towards them. Towards that violence of voice.
Such timidity of the abused. Not a murmur.
The vast crowd stolidly sit.
Shouting my words: 'Stop this bullying!'
No answers from anyone. Enormous silence. Heads turn.
Their eyes try to tell me more than meets the eye.
I turn on my heel and leave.
Better to have stayed away than to have arrived late.

THE BOY

The suffering was real.
The telling of it is simply a story.
How the child coped with the cruel events.

Hot shrapnels whizzed past.
Bombed buildings burst apart.
All around the town burnt.

Oil refineries, munition factories
but also tenements and buildings
human habitations cracked and burned around him.

The smell of death was everywhere.
That sweet, unmistakable smell.
The boy took no notice.

He walked from street to street.
He searched for his friends.
Bombers above him filled the sky.

They came so low
skimmed above the tops of tenements
the underbellies showed their horrid markings.

Yet the boy was undeterred.
It was his life not theirs.
The town was his town not theirs.

Hissing hot shrapnels missed him.
Buildings collapsed behind him.
Who let loose these mad devils?

Not that he was not annoyed.
Not that he was not angry.
Not that he did not curse the whole mad world.

He took no shelter just walked
among the ruins of the exploding town
stepping over the torn, cut open corpses.

And at last he reached his destination.
His uncle was by the furnace baking bread.
'I have come to help,' the boy said.

And all night they baked bread
neither of them would admit that the
whole town was forever dead.

TO MY MOTHER

Once more I was in mother's arms
Dead she was and could not speak
She was a fading memory
Something separate and only in my head
And being a poet or at least
A possessor of the poetic mood
At times of great stress
She was called into my thoughts
But could not materialise.
No doubt she is still waiting there
Waiting to recompose.
Her picture does not keep still
She looks older in my head
Than when I last saw her
A bit like my grandmother.
I cannot keep them separate.
But as I was saying
At the time of the latest war
In despair I wrote a poem.
A bad, hysterical, vindictive piece
Written with tears and abandoning sense
And this is what I said.

DECLARATION

I was one of them and they'd left me behind,
For time was their own and they had little space.
Now they are as far away in time as in space.
What was it they had objected to?
Perhaps they were as sorry as I am today,
For let me not pretend, I do miss them still,
although they were so cruel to me.
Your time will come, they yawned, but it is not yet
I poked at the fire while they snored in bed.
They were polite, icily polite, the Great Ones at whose feet I sat.
How many days and nights I have sacrificed just to be near them!
But if I had been blind or deaf or bereft of brains
Without a sense of smell or touch, it would have been the same.
They were great just seconds before I had entered the room,
As trembling legs took me upstairs to their presence,
had I but tip-toed so that they could not sense my approach,
so that I could have observed them as they really were,
but no, I never saw their greatness at all,
I saw blood, I saw love, I saw drunken stupor, that's all I saw.

UNDERSTAND THIS

What is there to say?
That which can be felt
Life is long – so much misery.
What can the meaning be?
To consider what has happened.
But this is new, this is not old
The place is different and so is the meaning.
You are here, not there
You are at home, because you are here.
Your life is here and now, not in the past.
What do they say in the Southern hemisphere
The ancient people there believe
The world travels towards them, not they toward the world.
Steadfast they watch over the waves till the wished-for island appears.
How am I to say with my Northern head and brain
That those in the Pacific are not in the right.
Therefore those that are homeless
Let them be proud of their exile
For where else can one live
Except in freedom, freely:
In the country of our own imagination.
But isn't that hurtful, isn't that insulting
That we cannot help everybody, everywhere
Those poor poor, those imprisoned
Those on the road, those persecuted, those on the run
Those who have been tortured, those that are tortured now
Those that have been murdered, those that the cold winds blew
Tossed like flakes under an evil sky
Through fire and through water.
But think of the children's sparkling eyes
Think of the mother's loving arms

Or think of those of whom nobody ever thinks
The old wrinkled faced grandmother
The weak, tired grandfather
Understand this, strength and coercion are not the same
And the world does not turn
Just for the sake of the rulers.

HIS WORLDLY GOODS

The sun was setting in the West
And a faint moon was still up in the East.
This was the day you spent with me.
We sat on a bench overlooking the lake.
You have grown so old, my friend,
So old and pale as the faint moon in the East.
But you pugnaciously straightened your back
And with your last strength you whispered:
'Here I am in my last moments.
When shall I ever see again
This sky, this lake, this sun.'
Hoarse was your voice, almost inaudible.
'What can I give you as a parting present
To you my life-long friend?
Not worldly goods surely
Of what use they are for me or for you
On this my certain, uncertain journey.
Best I leave you only my words
Let them sing in your head
And never from you depart
As contrarily now in good spirits I do so.'

So what could I do. I ran as fast I can
To the nearest hostelry and took out my notebook and pen
To write this down before I may forget
My great friend's passing words and gift to me.

Pondering over this with a beer and a fag
I couldn't believe my eyes, the door
Opened ajar and through it appeared
My old friend, hale and hearty as ever.

He marched up to my table
And looked at me very askance
Then he said with everyone to hear
'Give me back my words, you scrofulous scribbler!'

Was he right or was he wrong
Are these words his or are they mine?
Autumn has come, deterioration is everywhere
Falling leaves are here and words are there.

TERRA INCOGNITA

Bravely I press on,
Come on, comrades,
The sleepless dreamer totters in the mire
I hear the cracked sound of trumpets
And bravely I press on.
There is a cordial hostelry
At World's End
Where all things turn to nothing
We shall go and live there
There uncare is the same as care
Let us proceed bravely
Forward, comrades, forward.

ROBIN

for Emily

When robin sits on a branch
He sun shines
Through the tree tops

When you knock on my door
The sun shines
Through the windows

WHO DO WE ADORE?

One two three four
Who do we adore?
Where do numbers come from or go to in the dead of night
Have they been lurking before we came about?
How did we shepherd them into the daylight
Whoever planted them in earth and ocean in space and sky
How can there be room for them – where are their castles
When we are homeless are they homeless too?
Did somebody before we came about have prior knowledge of them
Or did we on a dull day invent them?
Have others unknown to us used them
In however a strange fashion.
But if it was one of us who brought numbers into the world
What insatiable urge drove us to share our beds and comestibles with them?
Do we need them more or less
Than we need the sweet sounds of music and the blushing buds of poetry?

GEORG HEYM'S BERLIN

Betarren Barrellen rollen from them Swellen
Their darklen schfire out the Tallten Shapen
The tugter tow ten ton. The dirtiest tailsnen
Hang grimig neath the oilygen Washen.

Two steamers comen with Musiken Maken
Horny chimneys throughen bridge-archen towen
Gruesome filthen stanken on riveren waven
The tannen tainten withen brownen skinnen.

The allen bridgen under whichen raften
Moven throughen ensounden the Hooten
Like which in dreamen arosen in stillen.

We letten loose and yearnen for Haven
To orcharden reachen. In thesen Idyllen
We observen giante chimnen, night lanternen.

HOWEVER ABSURD

Every moment is different
All we can hope for
Is that as each moment changes
However absurd we should still understand
Each moment's meaning
Pleasing or unpleasing.

THE POET OFFERS HIS WARES

I have four liners
I have four liners
I have four liners
I have four liners

Also have three liners
Also have three liners
Also have three liners

Plenty of two liners
Plenty of two liners

Working on one liner now

ANDREI CADRESCU

Here was a man who spoke in complete sentences.
Alas, one day, he was run over
By an even better articulated lorry.

THE RECKONING

On the first day of fame
His true love sent to him
An invoice for services rendered
Totting up the sums late at night
He could not find anything wrong
With the arithmetic.
So our hero packed his bags and departed.
To have stayed famous for two days
Was beyond his means

ADVERTISEMENT

I need an enemy
Everyone else has an enemy
Why haven't I got one?
Would you like to be my enemy,
If so send CV –
I am an equal opportunities employer
Apply in confidence

WHAT'S IN A WORD

I

The war is over – what a statement!
What war, when and whose doing?
Historians knock on my door
Newspapers are full of it
It's official, read all about it!
Peace is now the catch-word
Which puts a stop to war
I looked at the clock: it was quarter to four.
From war to peace, from peace to war
What an amazing transformation
Nation will not now fight nation
All is peace in love and war.
Rules are changing – codes are changing
The word of peace displaceth war
(*Enter entire Hungarian army, flags, trumpets*)

Chorus: Lay down your arms my friend
The war is over.
Peace, blessed peace is the new
Catch the new word

II

The war is over
Said my father
I was young and very poor
I was cold and thin and ill.
Such a thin little thing
I was in the land of dreams
Shuffling footsteps by my bedside
Second floor facing inward
Windows to the inner courtyard
Of a square-shaped tenement.
The war is over
It's official
Said my father
Can you hear the peaceful bell?
We were in the town of Pesth
Better known as Budapest
The country was called Hungary
A mis-spelling for Hungery
For many were hung in Hungary
Not a pretty sight to see
The war is over –
I rejoiced
Thank you father, my best doctor
Such news revives the dying,
White lies stuffed in downy pillows
Interesting story this

STONE UPON STONE

He must have been a generous man
Or forgetful man or a purposeless man
Who once lived in the Luxuryan valley

A cottage he built this generous man
Or a forgetful man or a purposeless man
And then he left the Luxuryan valley

He left his door off its hinges
He never closed his windows to the open air
His stone cottage now stands deserted in the valley.

On the hillside are the boulders from the ice age
Was he then also a generous man or a purposeless man
Or just a stone-hearted man

    that once lived in the Luxuryan valley?

THE DOOR

I worked for Herr K. in the last years of his life
By that time his doctors advised him not to speak
So as to conserve his energies.
They graciously allowed him to jot down his thoughts
And requirements on slips of paper.
The great writer and genius had very weak lungs.
He needed lots of fresh air and a clean room with flowers.
I tended to Herr K. and did his meals and tidied his rooms
I learnt quickly not to interrupt him at work
And never to move his papers,
So that he could find everything as he left them.
He had a great circle of admirers, both fellow writers and editors
Who were very eager to publish everything he had written.
I did read some of his stories after my work was done and although
I only had a modicum of education, I grew to admire him for his tenacity.
He was not very successful in his affairs with women.
He was too ill to entertain them. He was always very considerate towards me,
Although he never took me in his arms.
Once I asked Herr K. if there was any hope?
His eyes moistened as he quietly answered:
'There is hope, Frau K., but not for us.'

WAITING

Missing your train can either be a good thing
Or a bad thing or no thing at all.
There is frustration. A sense of displacement.
But perhaps it was a good thing
Like missing the Titanic.
The train you missed could have been derailed.
But then you could have got to your destination.
If you had a destination.
There is always another train full of people
Who either have missed the train before or
Happen to be on the right train.
None of them look very convinced or convincing.
They are either asleep or pretend to be asleep.
Some of them talk to themselves
Holding on to their ears. They are either in pain or not.
Or they could be worried that their ears might fall off.
When the train stops they rush for the doors.
They have either arrived or not arrived.
Whoever wound them up in the morning
Has done an excellent job.

ON THE PLATFORM

It is 11.38 and twenty seconds.
I can report truthfully that on the platform opposite
There are two benches and on each bench sits one individual.
There is no one else on the platform except for a rat
And a pigeon. The two individuals are about twenty
Yards from each other.
Nevertheless the fatter of the two grips his travelling bag,
Possibly worried that an eagle would swoop down from the sky
And carry his bag away. It would be too heavy for the pigeon.
The other, much thinner, individual looks comatose,
Or perhaps he is an actor practising the part of a man
Who is sitting on a bench looking comatose.
It is now 11.36 and twenty seconds.
Clocks on this platform go backwards.
At this rate the train I have just missed
Might come along any minute.

There are now two pigeons and no rat on the platform opposite.
How this transformation took place I have no idea.

THE WOULD-BE SHOEMAKER

I cannot cobble up other people's lives
To start with, I'm not a cobbler.
If I were a shoemaker
Which I'm not
I would probably construct a shoe
That nobody in their right mind
Would dare to walk on
For fear of instantly breaking its heel
Or clumsily smudge its mis-spelt soul.

UNDERSTANDING

The most we can hope for
Is that we might be understood by others
With different understandings to ourselves.

BIOLOGY

Adam Johnson (1965–1993)

A basketful of dead images floats across my mind, with contours blurred
Where once was your clear light, now signals total black-out and catastrophe.

THE JOURNEY

Last night I dreamt I was in Caribou
Which I always knew was my destination
The journey was long and heart-breaking
But I never stopped and I just carried on.

Last night I dreamt I reached Caribou
Which was my destination
A boy born out of no nation
At last reached his destination

But from my slumber I suddenly woke
By children's voices and birds' twittering noises
The day stood still, the air was motionless and cold
I stood where I have always been
And though through dream's eyes I have seen
This place was not my destination.

I turned to books and dusty shelves
Pored over maps with eyes so weak
I searched and asked yet none could I find
Where Caribou was – except in my mind.

Then exhausted I laid me down to rest
And in dream I beheld the boy that once was me
I had to run for he was so nimble and fast
And my grey beard was hindering me.

Please stop, I shouted, for old times' sake
Who else but you should know
The place the town I seek
Please stop I shouted for old times' sake
Give the poor man a break

And tell me for who else should know but you,
My younger self, the place the town I seek.

The boy stopped and grinned
Watermelon juice dripped down his chin,
Took me by the hand,
Slowly walked me across unfamiliar land
My playful younger self I knew what he thought

The boy and the old man could have found that place
If they would but search for their town
Boy, help me my boy for I have asked my friends all to tell me
Where is the crown of my home town Caribou?

The boy replied
'Go on and find
Some peace of mind…
For Caribou you shall never attain
The search is endless –
May you meet the friends you deserve
On night's long journey
Into day…'

YOU MIGHT HAVE NOTICED

A relatively new custom
May be observed in the polite circles
Of the town and the country
Is the habit of kissing both cheeks
Rather ceremonially as people meet
As a token of joy greeting friends.
Other customs such as rubbing noses together
Have lately fallen out of use.
But whatever, there is a lot of kissing
Going on at these polite gatherings
On the arrival of the guests in all their finery
Although it has also been observed
Not many of them do any kissing
On their departure.

THEN AND NOW

When nobody else
— so it seemed to me —
was saying anything
I spoke up and even
ventured to write
trenchant verse.
Now that everybody is talking
I just sit back and listen.

INTO THE STREET

Here I was tying my shoe-laces
Ready to go out
Here there is a fire where
My books surround me.
Out there the storm has stopped
No need to carry an umbrella
But it is cold and damp out there
Yet I must go out to visit two charmers
Who want my assurance
That their poetry is untarnished metal
And their cherries are juicy and sweet.
My father used to wear galoshes
To confront a day such as this.
My shoes are unpolished. No time to prettify.
I must hurry, my Muses are waiting.
I turn out the fire and step into the street.

SOME POETS ARE EVEN WORSE

Her feet went up to her knees
Broom in hand her two dogs watching
Sweeping the street from end to end
Peasant woman in a Kentish Town street.
'Please sir,' she said, 'did I hear ye aright'
She intoned in her incredible screech
And then I remembered who she was, the poet
Whom I once heard declaim a plaintive song
In a room above the old Engineer,
A curious tale about a maid in unrequited love
Pining for the gentleman above for whom she cooks and sews,
While around her sat the cognoscenti.
So at that moment of passing and impasse
I said politely that I would be favoured
With sight of her poems on the printed page
At this she screamed hysterically, denying their existence
That she was never a poet, never, never.
So, I said in passing, raising an imaginary hat,
May then Madam may I never
Compare ye to a summer's day,
'Never, unless me name be Seamus Heaney'

A MOAN ON A SUNDAY AFTERNOON

The birds sing, the aeroplane roars and squeals
The sun is shining, the drums are beating
Through closed eyelids the universe is red
Or a mishy-mushy hue, a confusion of orange and blue
And now like – the sun is gone –and yet shines again
Fixing and unfixing my moments like silver threads
And now the purest pink I ever saw
I mean green of the closest choicest weave.
Shining in a deep sea of red
I shall see them again,
Closing my eyes will make it happen.

What a jolly life you lead
Blink and unblink in your sleep.
The birds sing, good for them, aeroplanes roar now and then,
Down here it is much the same, never meeting old luck dame
The whole town is on the game

Quiet rivers of the mind
Take me where I do not mind
To the land that is yours or mine
Where all the milk is purest wine
Where the plants that gave me birth
Taught me sense and confidence
Quiet moments in the mind, where you hear the bells
The sound of alarm and of mirth
Where you hear the birds that do not sing
Where you hear the bells that never ring.

TOO LATE

I've told the truth to all who knew me
Now I know I have lied
For I told the truth when I was an adult
While truth only belongs to the child.

CONTAMINATED SOIL

I am sitting on a bench in London's Russell Square
Nearby is a walnut tree
Planted in memory of a 'freedom fighter'
The inscription on a stone gives his name and years
You were my friend and you went back to your homeland
To implant your seed of Freedom in its contaminated soil
You died there, who knows what became of your seed.
Here the tall healthy tree with its branches full
Now shivers in the breeze of the autumn air
And sends me a doleful whisper of a sound
Which forms into words in my nodding head:
Poor man, poor patriot, I told you so, freedom is here,
Stays here and always will be here.
Didn't I warn you, alas,
Freedom is not transportable

WORLD WAR TWO

My mother wore a paper shirt
My father wore a hat –
The metal albatrosses
Soon put a stop to that.

I see them faintly smiling still
And a bit surprised at that
For mother sweet was fond of her shirt
While father was at one with his hat.

But fate and destiny jointly declared
An unequal war on my mother's shirt
And their metal albatrosses
Destroyed my father's fine hat.

THIS IS NOT THE TIME

for Emily

This is not the time, still not the time
I said something two years ago
And am unable to repeat what I said

For they were first thoughts, true thoughts
When a particular pocket of time was measured in hours.

Other events have passed me by
Problems such as this was never the end of the world.

But it is there in black and white

And two years later I am still unable
To repeat what I said.

THE QUESTION REMAINS

Difficult to concentrate the mind
War has raised its ugly head
Populations are decimated
This is the rule of terror
And we live in its peaceful enclave.

There is food in the shops
The bars are full
The sun is shining
While our *raison d'etre* is cracking.
There are local difficulties
Our culture. Our way of life is
Eroded bit by bit.

Our books which contain all our precious thoughts
Are no longer treasured.

We are ruled by tyrants who despise our culture.
For it is the culture of peace.

The question remains:
How dare these people annoy us so?

What have we done to deserve such treatment?
How can we get these people off our backs?

NOTEBOOK IN HAND

Notebook in hand, pen at the ready.
He peers at a corner of a field
From the scented profusion he isolates a grass.

'Are you well', he asks benevolently.
The grass nods to the wind.

A month later, notebook in hand,
Pen at the ready, he returns to the field
The grass is still there and is still nodding.

Even though the wind has stopped
And despite the birds making an awful row
Which made conversation a little difficult
He felt happy enough until the grass stopped nodding.
Or if nodded, it was a curt nod, a polite nod.
He was made to feel unwelcome and went away.

A month later he went back to the same field
But could not get to the grass,
There were people everywhere, notebooks in hand,
Pens at the ready, cameras whirring and
The grass nodding to special wind effects.

CHAPTER ONE

All the years I have put meaning into my life, like cash into a bank –
isn't it time I should try to draw some meaning out of my life,
meritoriousness offers no rewards, to do one's duty,
to behave according to one's precepts
learnt from others – but to be one's own self and yet not leave behind
   one's principles,
oh the voice of cowardice, until all one's cowardice comes home and
here they are – interruption is called for.

CHAPTER TWO

What can I put in my travelling bag –
 shall I save from my yesterdays –
Oh how I hate luggage of any kind –
when you cannot read the words of
Ancient texts is it enough to admire their shapes –
leave it to luck, close your eyes and
Pick and pack things at random, then you can safely throw the lot away.
It is time I moved on.

CHAPTER THREE

This needs some explanation, not to mention imagination.
Some caterpillars cocooned in the lining of my breast pocket.
That happened, must have happened previously.
There in the room were my interrogators,
on long oak forms sat my jailers and
Future executioners. The president of the court coughed and whined:
'What have you got to say in your defence?'
I had nothing to say, but at that moment the cocoon opened and a
Multicoloured butterfly flew out of my breast pocket.
They all dropped dead and I walked out of my prison – a free man.
But in my hurry I left the butterfly behind.

CHAPTER TWO THOUSAND AND FIFTY SEVEN

'I remember a place where I was for ages. Somewhere. With some others.
Who knows for how long and in whose company.
It was always the same. Nothing ever altered. Nothing ever happened.
There was nothing for me to do. I didn't even breathe and nobody
    ever spoke a single word.
I was unable to move. The size of the place was sufficient for me.
Otherwise it was crowded. This persisted for many thousands of years.
That is, nothing happened. Without dreams, without thoughts, bodyless.
But I was there, somehow. If I had a mind or not, or some kind of feeling,
Hope or fear, that I do not believe now. The only thing
    that I remember is that
I was there, somewhere and for a long period of time.
I am convinced that
I was there right at the beginning,' he said.

MARTIAL SAID IT FIRST

Stop now, that's enough, stop scribbling
You cannot stretch this any longer
Others may proceed and urge you to continue
But you have covered enough paper already
They may not think the affair is over
But your book could have ended on the first page
Your readers are whining and are exhausted
Even your copytaker has said firmly
Stop your book writing, that's enough, stop.

RUNNING OUT OF INK

I think I have finally reached b. p.
All this travelling to put r. to r.
Always one step behind the g.t.
Inwardly a.
There does not appear to be much c.
But never will I g.i.
As for S.
To whom it may also a.
On the train to H.
For a little b.
Perhaps one day I shall return to L.
To collect my winnings in a l.
Which I cannot recollect ever e.

PROGRESS

I was born in enchanting Eastbourne
At the age of seventy-five
There I swore allegiance to her Majesty the Queen
In the presence of my lovely daughter
And two silver haired Maids of Honour.
So by chance and choice you may see me, comrades,
Dance and dance the anarchist monarchist polka.

THE LINK

Those in the know
Come in two sorts
Those who know something
They are one sort
Those who know nothing
That is another

TO AND FRO

Up the ladder climbs the little boy
He does this and that
Goes to and fro
Wanders here and there

Then one day he stops climbing
He still does this and that
Still goes to and fro
And wanders here and there.

But he is no longer a little boy
When he sees other children climbing the ladder
A certain tremor is stifled in his breast
Walks slowly on, shakes his head, amazed with amazement.

ART LESSON

—What is this man doing?
—He draws
—What does he draw?
—He draws us

—Is this what we look like?
—No, this is how he sees us.

A MOAN ON A SUNDAY AFTERNOON

There was a tribe in ancient days
A tribe of the charming people
How they prospered
Or how they lived or lived by
Or what they lived on
Was always a bit of a mystery.

The things they could do
These charming folk.
They had such funny names
And how charming were their mysteries
For what they knew was also their trade
And what they didn't know they practised nevertheless.

Many tribes have vanished into exile
More into oblivion!
Even this charming tribe is no longer what it was
For their enjoyable tricks
Have turned into nasty swindles.
Their mysteries are now embedded in code-books

But what happened to all those good people
Where are their caravans now
Where are their play houses
Where their charming customs
Those bonfires burning
Those peace pipes smoking?

THE MOMENT

This is the moment I've been waiting for
All these years of yearning
Through danger and horror
Surrounded by pitfalls
To reach that one moment
The moment I've been waiting for
That very special time
A moment would have been enough
Was that too much to ask
To keep this moment
But the moment I've been waiting for
and now it has come and gone
cold winds and hot
cascading rain
the mountains so high
ominous tranquillity
the enormous effort
where hardships endure
the cataclysmic clash
torrents and tempests
forever the turbulence
Has now come and gone

THERE WAS A TIME

There was a time when love alone
Permitted me a space of my own
The young thing was washed and cuddled
Kissed and caressed, pampered by all –
It was pleasant and oh so simple
The days went by and all was well
Never a rude word, but cakes with cream
The night was sleep, days were a dream.
Beautiful world, why did it end?
Love was a gift given freely
To be fought for in later years.
Slap on the face, punch on the throat
Broken shoulder, a cruel act
Poisoned knee, an accident.
An old woman, your grandmother
Gave you shelter of gentle love,
Your mother, darling, was beautiful
One loved you, not the one you loved,
Impossible now to recall
The snow, the rain, the years between
Have washed away all the traces
But the memory still persists
That was charmed time, halcyon days
Only marred by small surprises
A tear here then a smile there
Effect was all, its cause unknown.
The sun, the moon, the turning earth
The change of day was change of life
Each day's truth died by end of day
New patterns came, old patterns went
Related facts followed later
Never a full explanation

Even now I'm uncertain
Why and when did the magic cease
What and which bit holds the clue
Near civil war rages around me
While I debate my ghostly past
That was the time when love alone
Permitted me a space of my own
For me that space was paradise
For me that world is still alive

FOR THOREAU IN SORROW

Those who lead lives of quiet desperation
Oh, sacred August of falling apples!
Heed wisely Newton's gravitous explanation
Oh, the shock of the knock of delightful exhilaration.

ART AND THE MAN

The man in the garden was numbering the leaves
The tree was just a tree
The man was just a man
The numbering took ages

That was in the Summer
Every leaf was numbered
In the Autumn the man
Gathered the fallen leaves.

The man was in the garden pinning back the leaves
The tree was no longer just a tree
The man was no longer just a man
He was an Artist and his work of art was the tree.

WHERE IS THAT CHILD?

Where is that child that looked into the well
and threw a tiny stick and watched how fast it fell.
Deep was the well and as the splinter fell
the child saw the stick fall on a star in the deep well.

Deep was the well but now not even I can tell
where is that splinter that brought light to the well,
where is that child that saw the star in the waters of the well
or where was once that well not even I can tell.

NOW WE KNOW EXACTLY

The father was talking to the mother
Or the mother was talking to the father
It was difficult to tell which one was talking
In the end it came to the same thing anyway.

Their son or their daughter were listening
Or at least it looked as if they were listening
That humble look of theirs was some kind of proof
But it was difficult to tell.

What the father was saying to the mother
Or mother was saying to father
Was or could have been of great importance
To either son or daughter were they listening.

There were certainly words, weighty words,
Tentatively offered with care, love and attention
When the father hesitated the mother continued the thread
As the mother ceased the father continued.

Certainly either their son or their daughter were listening
And so they should. For one day soon it will be
Their turn to say these weighty things
To their sons and daughters should they be listening.

As for me watching them made my tears freeze into icicles
For it was a bit cold for this type of thing
Biting cold was the weather
As they were waiting for the ferry by the river nearly.

As they held their conversation
Amid the usual gunsmoke and the breaking of ice
Biting cold was the weather as they stood determined
By not what they said but by the manner of their listening.

WHY TWO?

On my way back from Austria a poem came to me in mid flight. I wrote the poem on a paper serviette. When I got back to England I couldn't find the poem and thought I had thrown it away. So I sat down and tried to remember the words and this is what I managed to salvage:

I am unable to advise anybody
About anything

There was a time when I thought
My opinion mattered.

Whoever put us here or
For what purpose is unclear.

'Carpe diem, quam minimum
Credula postero' said the latin.

Dishonesty is a trademark
Of ancient poets.

I am unable to express an opinion
Below or above the clouds.

UP IN THE AIR

Days later I was looking for a paper handkerchief to blow my nose on and suddenly found the poem intact on the serviette. It wasn't lost after all. Here it is:

There is nothing that I can say
That means anything at all
Over and above what
Everybody knows

I have no advice either to myself
Or to anybody else.
If there is a meaning
I haven't found it

There is no point to despair
As there is no point in feeling elated
I was here today: these words are mine now
Tomorrow there will be no trace of me.

Whoever and whatever have thrown us here
Have a lot to answer for.
Unless all creation is dumb –
Like myself.

I cannot choose between these two poems. Both are true – one is up in the air, the other down to earth.

IN THE MUSEUM

A long line of people in the park
Children and adults.
The line moved slowly
Only one person at a time
Went through the massive doors.
I felt like leaving, but didn't
John was somewhere in front
Reading a newspaper.
Pamela was polishing her nails.
I haven't had anything to eat
Susan was next to me, unconcerned.
Everybody I knew was there
I couldn't leave. Slowly we moved.
The trees were of a colour
Painters are fond of depicting
The crowd sang songs
No musician has ever written
This kept me amused.
Here I was in the park
And was nearing the entrance.
Those who have gone before
Were already inside the museum
Separated from us.
Susan gave me an apple
Which I ate with unconcern.
At last we reached the door.
I never carry anything
So they didn't search me.
The price of the ticket was scandalous,
I had to empty my pockets.
They refused a cheque for
The missing h'penny.

When I asked for a recount
The people behind me grew angry
And pushed down the barriers
They all entered with me
And nobody else paid
Although I still owe for the extra h'penny.
Everybody was now inside the museum
The rooms were packed.
I wanted to look around
But could not get near the exhibits.
John was still a little ahead
Still reading his newspaper
Pamela was putting mascara on.
Susan pulled me by the sleeve
And said: just look at this.
I had to hold her hand
For suddenly I felt frightened
For what I saw was my own home
Turned into a museum
Everything neatly hung and labelled.
'They have made me pay' I shouted,
'They have made me pay twice' –
First for the materials
Then for the exhibition.
All my life has been stolen from me
Paintings I have done years ago
The entire product of my life
All on the walls, in the glass cases.
John was still ahead
Reading the newspaper
Pamela was adjusting her hair
Susan pulled me towards

The far wall where hung
My favourite painting
Which was stolen from me years ago.
Just as I remembered it
The old chair and chess-board
With my favourite game clearly shown,
Just before the decisive move.
In a glass case my manuscripts
All those futile, meaningless words
Neatly indexed, deftly described
And I was not allowed to look
Not allowed to touch,
Unable to alter anything.
My works of art, my writings
They charged me to see them –
All stolen from me.
Susan was standing in front of a glasscase
She still looked unconcerned
But in the glasscase was a bead bag
Which once belonged to her
And now lay on green velvet –
An exhibit. The mouth of the bag was open
There they were, all her precious
Things and careful notes.
And drawings of furniture and flowers.
All this I only mention to show that I know
That everybody there, especially Susan,
Was robbed, of our things, of our thoughts
And then made into an exhibit.
This was the new catch.
All that multitude gawping to see
Their own lives, neatly indexed,

Accredited, catalogued.
The red and black period, circa 1968.
John was still a little ahead
Reading a newspaper.
Pamela examined her nails critically.
Susan and I were the last to leave.
What I love about her is that she is still unconcerned,
Whereas the very thought of it makes me hot with rage.
As for John not only has John disappeared
But also all that knowledge he gleaned from his reading.

H'ONOPONONOPONO

Be patient oh soleski Joyceski for now I have other fish to fryski
I must speak of H'-, the train at this station is standing at H'-
I'm not sure that I got the spelling right but H'- was the name of my departed
Friend and fellow writer, an author well-respected in his family circle
But otherwise little known. I was certain that he was a writer because everybody
Who knew him was full of his praises. Apart from his name I haven't myself
Read anything by him. Unless the family will collect together his manuscripts
Who knows how many masterpieces among them
will ever be in the public dimension.
At the moment I'm in such low spirits as a writer that I was even contemplating
To write a novel about my cat, surely even worse than writing books about dogs.
This is the moment that every writer dreads.
I have decided to follow in the footsteps of H'- and write his collected works myself.
There can be no objection from H'- he is well and truly gone.
As for his family, I do not need them whatsoever. After all I have known H'-
All my life and had the privilege of observing him at every stage of his life,
Although I never caught him wielding a pen.
He came in all sorts of guises and sizes from toothless little infant
To toothless old man. Every time I met he looked totally different.
'Is that you, H'onopononopono,' I ask
And he replies: 'Who else could I be?'
He could easily have been somebody else.
And now he is gone. Frequently people come up to me and ask:
'Who are you?' And I reply
'I'm the new H'onopononopono, as good as the last one,
The great departed author H'-'
Everybody is delighted. I hear them murmuring
'Such an artistry, such grace, a great writer, the wisdom of centuries
Under his lofty brow'. A great encouragement to continue in my task.
I decided to divide H'-'s work into sections.
First volume: published work
Second volume: unpublished work.
In the circumstances it will be better to start with the unpublished work,

For hitherto there is no work that is published.
As for his unpublished work
That will also have to wait
Until I have time to sit down and compose it.
Next Thursday I may have five minutes at least to write a couple of sentences.
Perhaps I shall start with an evocation
Or at least a nod in that direction.
What I dread most is that H'- is not gone at all,
just taking a long time in the toilet.
Then what will I do, he might look me in the eye and say:
'How can you impute such thoughts to me,'
and there he is with his entire family, who do not even notice me.
And there is no room to swing a cat
Never mind writing a novel about her.
So good-bye H'- it was good to know you, at least for a little while.
Console yourself: Perhaps great writers never die,
Especially if there remains nothing to remember them by.

FOREIGN LANGUAGES

All languages are foreign.
There are some languages however
Which sound more foreign than others.
There is no need to be annoyed unduly.
The chances are that if you parachute
Out of a burning aeroplane
Even if you are not swallowed up
By inhospitable waves but hit the ground safely,
The first person you will meet will demand
Some proof of identification in a language
Which nobody in their right minds would wish to speak
Never mind understand and have a cosy chat in
About prepositions ending a sentence with.

Translations from the Hungarian of Attila József

COUNTRY OF THE DEAD

The barley grows for his lordship
Fearful flies the pheasant in his woods.
The lake is his, and under winter's ice
It is for the sake of his lordship that the good fish hide
To survive in the mud.

TWO FRAGMENTS

As if I had been looking
For a hundred thousand years
And only now see, suddenly.

★

The poet is the engineer
Of the world's magic.

SAFFRON

i.m. Apollinaire and Miklós Radnóti

Now the meadow sprouts poison and flowers till late autumn
The cow chews the cud
And is slowly poisoned
The meadow saffron is blue and lilac
Your dozy eyes are the colour of this flower
Just as their petals are blue
Just as this autumn
And gazing into your eyes my life is slowly poisoned.

A pack of schoolboys run riot about the meadow
Their cloaks billow while music resounds
And they tear at the flower that is both mother and daughter
That have that hue of eyelids
Which colourlessly flap in fear
As the flower is shaken by the force of the wind

The stubborn herdsman softly and silently sings
While the grazing cattle wail and bellow
As they steamingly leave forever
The great meadow which is preparing to die.

Based on translations from Miklós Radnóti

YOUR COOL LIGHT

for Susan

Be good to her, for she is your love
She stood by you many a year
While others have given you up for dead
She warmed your heart and held your hand
She is your cool light in the midst of all fear.

For I loved you more than all that I know
You are grass and tree and wind and sky
You are more than me for I am but flesh, bone and hair
But you dear love is what a being immortal shape
I always thought myself to be, but it is you not I.

For life is your embrace, your impatient smile
You are bird and fish and snake and tim'rous mouse
Lie now on my faithful arm oh my love
My love for you is the perpetually moving machine
The ancients left us lovingly in the lumber of this house.

PERHAPS

If you think there is nothing
then you have nothing to say
If you think there is something
then you have something to say
and if you think of honour
you will have something
honourable to say.

There were those people –
I'm talking of the past –
when there was still a choice
of occupation.
The word itself is an indication
as to the choice.
There were those whose occupation
was the occupation of territories
and there were those
whose occupation was work
small tasks slender hopes
in and on and for and with
their peopled land.

There was always a conflict
over the meaning of words
nobody ever agreed
except in groups of languages
certainly there were words in abundance
all those languages
each discussing the same
and each in their own language
nobody ever agreed
except in groups of languages.

So there was this word
occupation.
There were two languages
which misunderstood
each other's definition.
One said – right, I occupy,
let them work,
that's their lookout.
I'll take all their produce
by force or by hook
or by crook.

So some were forced
and some were crooked
and some were hooked.
The more abundance was produced
the more the occupiers took
the more the people worked
the more they got exploited.
Frequently they changed sides.
All because of a word with two meanings.

But even in those days
There were people
who were honourable.
Such a person, by what I hear,
was the poet Catullus who once
addressed Caesar
in the following lines:
Nil nimium studio, Caesar, tibi velle placere
nec scire utrum sis albus aut ater homo.
He had no desire to please Caesar
or wanted to know him at all.

ADDRESS UNKNOWN

Mother, they are killing each other,
Death is everywhere.
The language you taught me
It's useless, mother, their bombs
Have made me deaf.
And I live among the living dead.
Otherwise, everything is alright
And I have some wonderful friends
But it looks to me
Something might be done about
The state of the world

TONGUE-TIED

If the news should ever come to you, Emily,
Of one of two kinds:
That I had ever been false to you,

Or that I'm no more among the living,
Will you put grief aside and love me still?

AFTERWORD

Art and the Man

John was born Réthy János in December 1930 in Budapest to a theatrical family. His mother Ilona Shaffer had been a performer and his father Istvan and uncle György were running the Hungarian Theatre Agency founded by his grandfather in 1882. Two of his uncles were literary journalists, his great-aunt was an opera singer and great-uncle an eminent mathematician. As a little boy he was sent to an English language nursery school and thus learnt only English nursery rhymes.

The family's names had been buffeted by regulatory changes over the past half century – from Rothbaum to Réthy. In 1942 John's grandfather Lipot was taken to court by an aristocrat because only Hungarian aristocrats should be allowed to have an 'H' and 'Y' in their names. So the family was left H-less and Y-less and John Réti arrived in London with his name mangled, anglicised and reversed.

The Réthys were Jewish enough to be persecuted by fascists but culturally or religiously Judaism did not have much of a presence in Jánci's childhood. During the war John's mother had him confirmed as a Catholic in the hope that it would provide some form of safety. John would say he was allergic to religion. John's maternal grandfather disappeared during a pogrom in Serbia, from which his grandmother escaped by swimming the river Drava with her two little children on her back.

Many of John's poems refer to the Second World War. These touch lightly, delicately sometimes as if a word or two of fact were as much as was possible to write of the reality. One must realise that they do describe very literally the awful impact on his childhood of the war and the siege of Budapest. The family was separated: mother, father, grandmother, János all hiding in different places – cellars, lofts, bathhouses, and János being the one who went between them carrying news. There were corpses in the streets, in the swimming pool. János's father and uncles were put in internment camps. He visited his father and talked to him through the fence, thinking to persuade him to climb out while the guards were watching football, his father's refusal and fear to do this had a profound impact on János. His beloved uncles disappeared – Uncle Lajos who gave him a fountain pen and encouraged him to be a writer. John never spoke of the transportations but they are referred to in the lines '(the new jews)/On the last train to Dachau'.

John's most terrible experience in the war was the death of his maternal grandmother who had been his main carer before the family was split up. 38,000 civilians had been killed in the six weeks of the Siege of Budapest and yet the core of his family had survived. The day 'peace' was declared his grandmother spoke out of concern to a very young Hungarian soldier. She advised him to take off his fascist armband since the Soviet troops were taking over. He shot her in the head. When John was told he ran weeping through the streets.

John was a pacifist. War was an impossible solution to anything. When he was sixteen he wrote a play about the war and how the adults had ruined the world for children. He got his friends to perform it on the steps of the Parliament building. His father had received veiled threats from the Communist authorities when he went for permission to reopen the Hungarian Theatrical Agency. Perhaps because of the play or perhaps because he saw that it would not be easy for János under communism, his father, in 1947, used his theatrical connections with the British Council to obtain a very rare travel permit to Britain, sponsored by the Labour MP John Parker.

Days before his seventeenth birthday John left Hungary on the Alberg Express for a winter holiday with his aunt in England. Without realising it he had become a stateless person. Again and again through his poems there is the refrain of displacement. His aunt burned his passport and there was no way back.

John had thought he would be going home to University in Budapest. He declined his aunt's plan that he should study at Pitman's Secretarial College, London. Nevertheless he later taught himself enough to translate Latin and Greek in poems and read Anglo-Saxon and Hebrew poetry and the roots of English Literature. A Roman said of the people of Pannonia (later Hungary) that they were *stultus* or thick. *Ulysses*, *The Romany Rye* and *Tristram Shandy* were the books that John always returned to.

All games enchanted John. He learnt chess as a child and played in competitions throughout his life. 'Why Two?' was written on the return journey from playing for the British Seniors team in Austria. Through these poems there is the Lewis Carrollian delight in language games and plays on words. The nonsense, wisdom, satire, mathematics and language of Carroll were very dear to John.

At seventeen he became apprenticed to a Czech publisher, Mr Prager of Lincolns Prager and learned the craft from him. He then plunged into Soho bohemia and published young writers in his little magazines *The Cheshire Cat*, *Intimate Review*, *The Fortnightly* and wrote his novel of the bohemian experiences, *Supersozzled Nights* in 1951. The poem 'Declaration' hints at the discomfort of being a foreigner on the English literary scene.

For several years in the 1960s John was an editor of the anarchist paper *Freedom* – there is something of this in the poem 'Freedom'. He also was deeply involved in the political squatting movement of the late '60s and early '70s. Resistance to the powerful property magnate Joe Levy in Camden Town ended in his own family's eviction and loss of home and livelihood.

In the 1970s John went to the City and Guilds Art School and became a painter. Some years later nearly all his paintings were stolen. He didn't paint again. Some images he tried to recover in sketch books. Maybe some became poems, certainly there is film making and performance art in his poetry.

In 1982 John and his partner Susan and myself, their daughter, were given the keys of a building in Torriano Avenue owned by Camden Council. It became a temporary home, and then Torriano Meeting House evolved out of their common interests. They played host to the writers of the '50s once again – John Heath-Stubbs,

Stephen Spender, Bernard Kops. And host to striking miners' wives, cabaret performers, antiwar groups, musicians, playwrights, artists; host to dreamers and utopians of the Stonehenge Campaign. John began to publish poetry again under the imprint Hearing Eye, poets from the old days and new people that came through the door. In this collection there are memories of some of these – Arthur Jacobs, poet and Hebrew scholar whose work John perhaps respected above all others; Harriet (Bee) Cutler, a playwright, who ran the Lantern Theatre, a sister venture to Torriano Meeting House in many ways; Madge Herron in 'Some Poets Are Even Worse'; György Krassó, Hungarian dissident; John Gravelle, teacher and talker, who reads his newspaper throughout 'In the Museum'.

John was stateless until 2007, when he was obliged by international changes to choose a state, Hungary or Britain, because it became impossible to travel abroad without a national passport. They said that it was no longer permissible to be stateless. The Hungarians wouldn't have him because he couldn't prove he was a Hungarian. He evaded the Britishness test but in the end acquiesced to swear allegiance to the Queen because, he said, she, like himself had experienced war in her youth. He was surprised to find that an insecurity about belonging that he had never realised was there, lifted. After the ceremony he said that he was born again in Eastbourne.

Emily Johns, January 2012

Poems taken from the following sources:

New and Unpublished Poems

Then and now
Six grand rooms
Stone upon stone
To and fro
Two incidents
The would-be shoemaker
The link
Advertisement
Running out of ink
The Moment
Why two?
Up in the Air
How myths are born
For Thoreau in Sorrow
Racing News
Saffron
Alas

Useful to know
The geographer
Foreign languages
However absurd
The Good Shepherd
For Susan
Contaminated soil
Terra Incognita
His worldly goods
Into the street
Progress
Some Poets Are Even Worse
Monsters
Understand this
Top of the morning
Know this
Robin

Song of Anarchy and other poems (1984–1988) (Hearing Eye, 1989)

Conversation
A Moan on a Sunday Afternoon
What's in a Word
Tenant
Declaration

There was a Time
Your Cool Light
The Journey
Freedom
Vision at 12.30 am

Touching the Sun: poems in memory of Adam Johnson by some of his friends (Hearing Eye, 1995)

Biology

In the Museum, Poems (1993–2003) (Hearing Eye, 2007, incorporating *What's in a Word* and *A Stranger Here*)

In the Museum
To die in Madrid
To my Mother
Address unknown
Art and the Man
Note book in hand
Georg Heym's Berlin
World War Two
The poet offers his wares
The Reckoning
Now we know exactly
You might have noticed
The kitchen chair
Chapter One
Chapter Two
Chapter Three
Chapter Two Thousand and Fifty Seven
Too late
Understanding
This is not the time
Tick Tock
Perhaps
The cherry tree
Country of the dead *and* Two fragments by Attila József
Mourn
Vir stultus sum
Tongue-tied

The best of all possible words (Hearing Eye, 2008)

The Boy
The Door
Work
The question remains
Art Lesson
Martial said it first
Ponderment
Homageiski to authoriski of Ulysseiski
Who do we adore?
H'onopononopono
That was that
Andrei Cadrescu
Waiting
A moan on a Sunday afternoon
On the platform
Where is that child?
The meaning of life

Books available from www.hearingeye.org

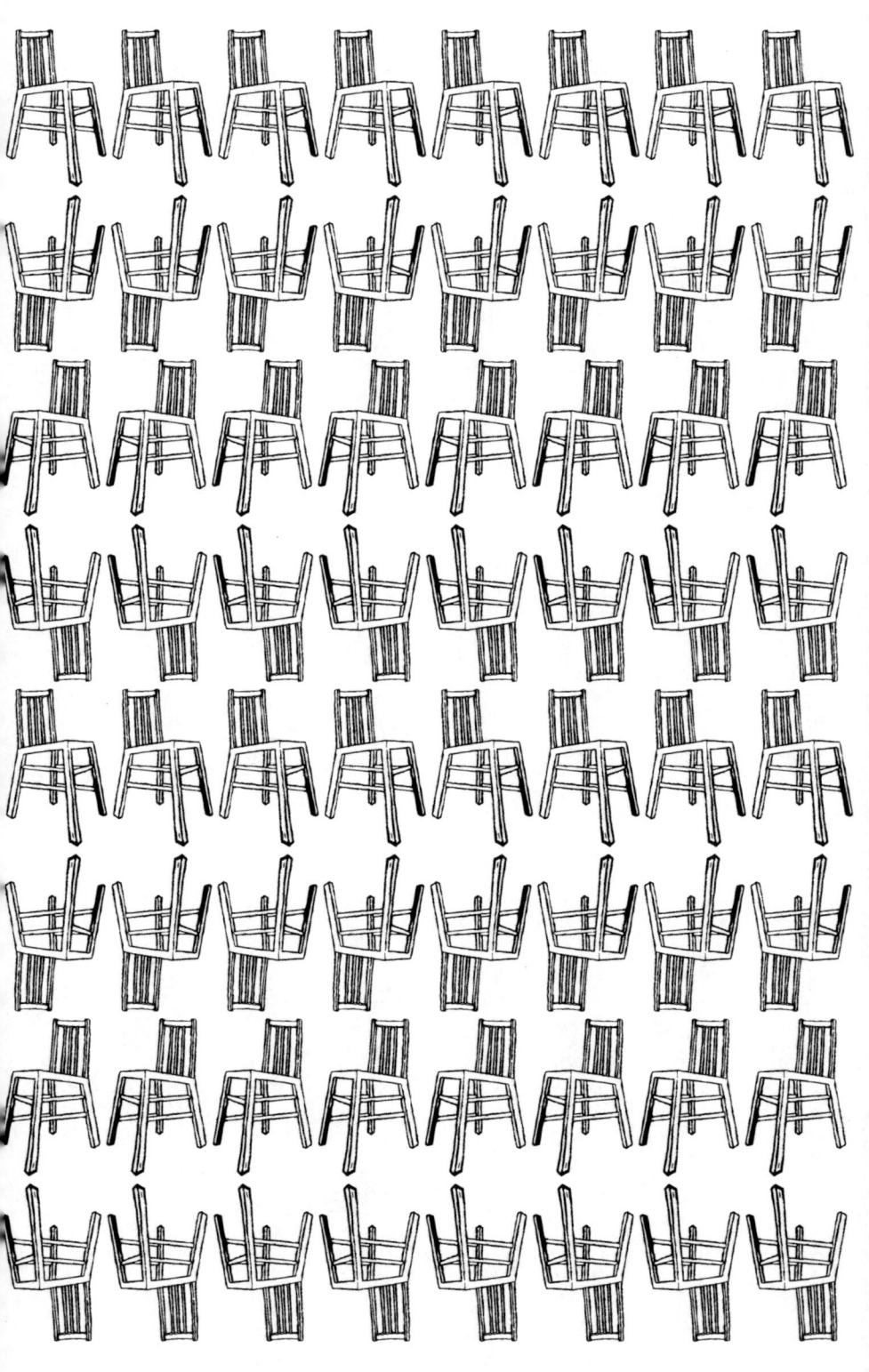

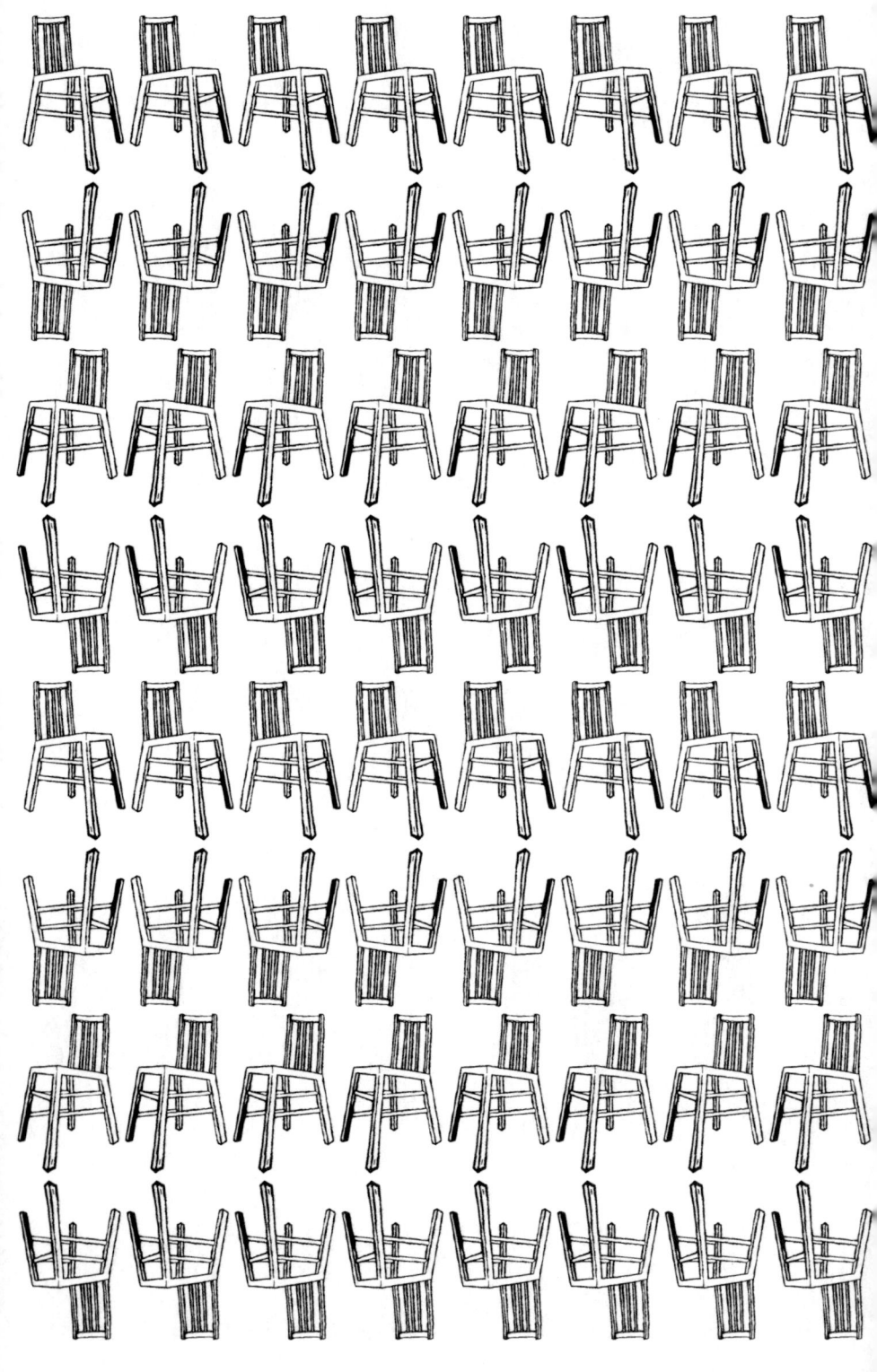